411 . . . The Terrorists Within

Dear Joe,
A pleasure
to meet you. Thank
you for inviting me
to the book signing.

Janie

411 . . . The Terrorists Within

A cancer story

Janie Chenevert

To order additional copies of this book, contact:
Xlibris Corporation
1-888-795-4274
www.Xlibris.com
Orders@Xlibris.com
51240

I dedicate this memoir to all my family, friends and care givers who took the journey through cancer with me. I thank you all for your support, prayers, cards, calls and caring.

I could not have battled these "terrorists within" without your backup.

This is also dedicated to all cancer survivors and their families.

Preface

This is another story of a cancer survivor. It recalls some of the agony and memories of dealing with the procedures and feelings of one going through the cancer ordeals. A rollercoaster of emotions befall the survivor and their loved ones.

It is important to know that this is a major disaster affecting the several lives involved with a survivor. The survivor is the "star" in the play but there are many important roles that support the "star".

Spouses, children, parents, siblings, friends, doctors, nurses, counselors, social workers, and many others lend to the survival of the "star". Physical assistance, care and "warm fuzzies" are given as needed, in most cases. Mental support and endurance is just as needed and given by professionals and friends on a regular basis.

The mental state is a major factor in the physical progress of the survivor. Spiritual support is one of the essential factors in both mental and physical well being.

PART I

October 2003

It was a clear, hot day, everything was going moderately well, I was unusually happy. Then WHAM!! I was hearing, "There is something suspicious on your mammogram—we want you to take another". Where is the foxhole? Where are my weapons?? Maybe it's a false alarm—it just can't be!! Wait for the results of the next mammogram. Probably just scar tissue.

Four years ago I faced the same terrorist attack. Only that time I had a warning—I found the lump. Neither the mammogram or the doctor knew. Should I tell them or let them use their informants, their spy machines to locate and seek the terrorists themselves? No, I better give them the 411 (*information*) or the terrorists might do something terrible, irreversible!

The war was about to begin again—no camouflage would protect me, no tanks to roll in and bomb these bad boys. I would have to fight with a small, but mighty, army. Thank God for my army of family, doctors, nurses, social workers and fellow survivors.

My first war, in 1999, was basically arming myself with information. The first contact, ACS (*American Cancer Society*), find out what they know, amazingly a LOT. They speedily sent a wealth of information, my arsenal was building. Friends at work gave me the scoop from survivors of previous wars and surgical procedures. They scanned the internet—the highway of information, and brought more secret policies.

I couldn't believe what I was up against. The torture and the medical submission I'd face. The mental anguish, the strength to not succumb but to fight harder than I ever had to fight and not give up or wave the "white flag" of surrender. I had to call in God's army, the big guns. "Help me Lord, I can't do this on my own! I need you to give me your super power. I need you not only to

help ME in this fight, but to send an army of angels to protect my family and friends during my flight to war. I can't be there for them, I have a war to fight. Please send backup, SOS".

Little did I know God was already in action, he calmed me, set me in motion, sent information, special angels and His special peace. I was ready to fight.

Armed with information I faced the commander, the oncologist. "What am I up against, what strategic maneuvers are possible? Should I wipe them out or use the conservative route?" After consultation, I went to the 2nd in command—the surgeon. I just had to hear it confirmed again and let it sink in—CANCER is not an easy digestion. Knowing you have it but still hoping against all odds—maybe not. It may sound stupid, but denial is ever powerful.

Well, the big decision: lumpectomy, mastectomy, or bilateral mastectomy—what to do? After consultations, talking with survivors, mind searching, common sense and praying for a miracle the decision must be made. Through research, it's stated that a lumpectomy can have the same effect as a mastectomy, your body is not as disfigured but you must have radiation. A mastectomy is final—no radiation or chemotherapy, if the lymph nodes are clear. With a mastectomy you just have surgery, no more treatment but you are left with one breast. Bilateral mastectomy—no breasts, no more treatments BUT even with both breasts gone, cancer can still reoccur! Those nasty terrorists—they can strike without warning. I hate them!! All the ammunition in the world is no protection, no guarantees, no finalization.

After careful consideration, the decision of mastectomy of my left breast is made, final answer. However, the doctor asked that I seriously consider a lumpectomy. Think it through—if cancer comes back it would have something to attack beside my lymph nodes, bones, blood or other areas. "Ok, I'll consider." That night I thought, I prayed, I consulted with my husband—MASTECTOMY—this will give lesser chance of reoccurrence, no further treatments. Prosthetics would keep me balanced and visually acceptable. After calling the doctor's office the next morning to notify his nurse of our final decision, we were prepared for surgery.

Surgery day started off smooth. My husband, mother, sisters, son, sisters-in-law and their husbands were at the hospital for support. It was like a party—no time to think of the operation; THEN I'm called to the pre-op nurse. "Hi Janie, I see you are here for a left breast LUMPECTOMY." "NO!" I said, "A left breast MASTECTOMY!" The nurse explained her papers stated lumpectomy and had to consult with the doctor's office for a decision. Confirmation of left breast mastectomy was cleared. I saw the surgical nurse, anesthesiologist and

surgical assistant—each asked the exact question. "Are you here for a left breast lumpectomy?" "NO", I replied each time, "a left breast mastectomy." I stated, "Give me a marker so I can write it on my chest!" Everyone laughed and said, "All the papers are now in order, a mastectomy was what I would get". HA, no such luck!! A lumpectomy was performed and get this; the doctor was cleared, no litigations could touch him, even after he admitted he did not read the chart before surgery. His nurse got fired because she verbally did not inform the doctor even though she noted the change in the chart. Go figure the justice here.

The lumpectomy meant I had to have radiation, HORROR. The nurse questions me: "When you go in the sun do you tan or burn?" "I burn", I replied. "Well expect the same extent during radiation". I was introduced to the radiation doctor, shown the rooms and equipment, and given a start date for the treatments. After the third treatment I was badly burned, I mentioned it to the nurse and showed her the area and asked if there was anything I could do to help alleviate the burn and the pain. She suggested I see a dermatologist because "You couldn't be that burned on just the third treatment. You are just probably allergic to a new soap . . ." NO NEW SOAPS USED!! Two weeks wait to see the dermatologist—no allergy, it was the radiation. Treatment continues, I continue to burn. When there were only three treatments left, the technician speaks to the doctor to see if I can get a break. I tell them no, they should have given me a break earlier, not when I only have three more treatments "FINISH".

Badly burned, miserable and in much pain I finished radiation. "WHEW, I made it, I'm done." Let's get on with my LIFE. Surprisingly I healed quickly and smoothly, thank God. First visit the oncologist: "Have you considered chemotherapy?" To myself I shouted, "ARE YOU NUTS!! I have 1 1/2 tits, an armpit that looks like a bomb exploded or a forest fire ravaged it when I could have had a mastectomy and no follow up treatments." "No, I have not considered CHEMO!!" my mouth said. "Why do I need chemo? I was told with the lumpectomy and radiation I would not need chemo. Is there more cancer? Will chemo increase my chances of not getting cancer again?" I was given a 5% better chance of not getting cancer again. "No, I don't want chemo unless it's a sure cure". No guarantee, no chemotherapy. Next visit to the oncologist, "Have you considered tamoxofin?" "What's tamoxofin, how does it increase my lifespan or decrease the chance of cancer reoccurring. What are the side effects?" I asked. "The side effects are: hot flashes, vaginal bleeding, loss of eyesight (which I am already battling), chance of cervical cancer, etc., etc." the oncologist replies. "No thanks, I have too many problems with medication, and I don't want to exchange one cancer for another. I know breast cancer can be caught early enough for treatment. Cervical cancer, on the other hand, is more deadly. "I THINK NOT," was my answer.

Ok, decision made, was it the right one, should I cave in and have more treatments—ARE THE TERRORISTS STILL AT BAY?

Each oncologist appointment was scarier that the previous, every three months. Finally, the doctor says, "How would you like to come back in 6 months?" 'THANK YOU GOD!" "Yes, that's good news, thanks, see you in six months." Mammograms every six months for the left breasts. OWEE. OWEE. At last the doctor says, "See you in a year." Hallelujah!!"

Put the camouflage away, put all the ammo in safe keeping, breathe in a deep sigh of relief. Everything looks bigger and brighter. Everything tastes good. This is better than any day I've had in years. YES!!

A whole year with no doctor's appointments. Three years, mammos good, see you in a year!! YES! The fourth year, I was great! I went to my annual mammogram with confidence—a few days later I get a call followed by a written report. "The mammogram showed something suspicious, don't worry, more times that not it proves NOT to be cancer. Can you come in for another mammo?" When I go back, they ask to get film from last years mammo to compare. The mammo I take shows the same "suspicious image". A biopsy is required. NO, this can't be happening again. I never felt a lump; the doctor never felt a lump. "Why put me through a biopsy when there is NO LUMP?" It must not be true, I don't want any unnecessary procedures. I ask if this biopsy would be an incision, like the last one, or a needle—I know a needle biopsy usually doesn't come back as cancer. My sisters and friends had needle biopsies—all benign, some needed aspirations only. A ray of hope! The doctor says it will be a needle biopsy.

Ok, I can do this. He explains the procedure. I lie face down on a table with a hole in it. The breast is put in the hole and lidocaine is injected for pain. Then a "wide" needle will be inserted at the site with the help of x-ray and injected several times until the needle gets a "clean" tissue sample. (I had five injections.) This procedure was very stressful. The nurse put a "gelly" ball in my hand to squeeze for stress relief. I burst the ball. The gel went everywhere! After the procedure, instructions and a warning. "Watch out for bruising". After the second day the bruising started—they forgot to mention PAIN. I was sore and bruised for over a week.

The biopsy showed the "terrorists from within" were at work again. CANCER in the opposite breast. I thought it was reoccurring, but "lucky" me. A brand new cancer and a different type. The first cancer was "ductual" and the BRAND NEW cancer was "lobular". The good thing is it can be treated as a first time cancer. All options were possible. If you have radiation on one

side you can't have it again on that same side. The new cancer can be radiated if I choose a lumpectomy. Chemo is an option. Mastectomy, lumpectomy—all options—LUCKY ME!

Not lucky me, how can I be lucky . . . THEY'RE BACK! I'm not prepared to fight. I don't want to fight!! All the strength, life and hope is gone. I can't do this! I can't face this—not again. It's not my time, I don't want anyone else to have it; ok, what do I do?? I can't think—my brain's dead—my eyes won't stop pouring, my heart will break it hurts so bad. I don't want to go on. "Please let me sleep—sleep, maybe it's a dream—maybe I won't wake up!! Maybe when I wake up it won't be real. Sleep, sweet sleep, heart stop beating so I can sleep, I need rest".

Well, I wake up and it's real! The war has begun. I'm not ready! I don't want to play. I want no part of this CANCER thing.

As I write it is two weeks before surgery. A bilateral mastectomy—I hope I'm ready for this. I made my decision based on the fact I don't think I can endure radiation again (well, I could if necessary)—I probably can endure anything as painful as it might be (mentally and physically). I know God will help me endure but I just plain old don't want to. Chemo is not a 100% cure and a mastectomy will lessen the chance of reoccurrence.

Wipe out these invasive terrorists. This time I have just my family for support. HA. They're concerned, but their lives go on—I'm just an obstacle, a land mine in their view, "walk carefully, she might blow". DAD GUM RIGHT I might explode! I'm loaded—what I need is someone to REALLY understand. There is the support group—they're great but I see them 2xs a month. There are my friends where I used to work. They all say call, they're all concerned—many people are praying. I'm so grateful, I'm so blessed but I feel so burdensome. Others tell me of their family outings, weddings, graduations, vacations—all I can tell them is of my doctor's appointments. I want to give some great news—I don't want prayers, I want to pray for others but I don't want to pray for recoveries. I want to pray for good health and good things. I want rainbows, pretty fields of flowers, bubbling brooks—NOT CANCER.

The closer it gets to the actual surgery, the crankier I get. It takes me in unsuspecting moments—I snap at a family member or clam up. It's hard for me to listen to people's everyday trials. It's as if no one knows I'm screaming inside, "HELP ME!" I feel like the "FLY" trapped in the spider's web—"HELP ME, HELP ME!" But, there is nothing anyone can do—no one wants to hear my pleas. "It'll be ok, you are a survivor." "I can't believe how good you're taking this." "I don't think I could

do as good as you are doing." Well look at me—I'm falling apart." I'm not doing well! I just can't let it out—it's trapped, I'm trapped, the terrorists within have me captive—my hands are tied, my feet are shackled—I can't just run away!

I try to keep busy—make costumes for the grandkids—help with school reports—"get your mind off yourself, you can do it old girl, after all you are strong." I know everyone I know has my best interest at heart and in their prayers. I am truly appreciative. My brain knows what's happening—I know I have to go through this. I know I can go through this, I will survive. I will be ok.

I have great faith in my Lord and His Son, Jesus Christ. I have never been let down, I am truly Blessed even with all the disparities in my life. I've never been denied anything I've ever asked for that I truly wanted. Anything I didn't get I truly did not pursue because of timing or someone else's needs. I regret my strength is not as it should be, I regret my faith is not as strong as I want it to be and not as strong as it should be or as strong as He deserves it to be.

I'm struggling to understand why I must endure these terrorists another time—I guess I missed the calling the first time. I get so many messages I can't decipher what it is I'm supposed to get or do out of this.

Things seem so surreal—nothing seems to have purpose—why does one struggle all their life to do the right things: care about people, animals, plants and have these terrorists enter and take all the meaning away . . . WHY??

Where can I go to get the answer? I know the answer and I know people, animals and plants are all beautiful, necessary and meaningful—I just need some assurance. I just need a sense of normalcy, but things will never be "normal" again. I am sure, just as the first time, I'll have the surgery and eventually my brain and my heart will see things in prospective. I will have beauty, calmness, peace and a place again in this crazy, unreliable and wonderful world. The terrorists will continue to strike and bring turmoil to someone's life and I and others, not involved, will try to forget they exist.

Some people will be Blessed to never know these terrorists within. Those who know or know someone who has experienced them will become stronger and always armed, hopefully, for nothing more that the average cold.

—end part I—

Part II

Before I start with Part II, I would like to clear up a few issues. I definitely do not want to give, or leave, the wrong impression of my wonderful support groups.

My family consists of a husband, who did not deal with illness or death . . . it is too hard for him to witness anyone he loves go through any pain or suffering. He mustered all he had to try to help me through this, mentally and physically. My children, a daughter and a son, were very concerned, helpful and supportive. My granddaughters were at the age they knew something was very wrong and were very apprehensive. I had to constantly reassure them I'd be fine and they, too, were helpful and very thoughtful. All of them a bright spot in my life.

My mother and sisters were very much concerned, thoughtful and supportive as well as my in-laws, relatives and friends. My co-workers for the first part (I was still working) was just as family. My brother and his family showed concern and were thoughtful also.

I do not, by any means want to undermine all the strength and support I needed to endure this war. It was shown and given to me freely with warmth, sincerity and faith. I could not have faced this ordeal alone. I am forever grateful.

OK—take a deep breath, here goes the second bout. The school district where I worked decided to change insurances so in the mist of the news of the reoccurrence, I had all new doctors, a new hospital and all new testings. In a way, this was probably a good thing.

This whole new battle had all different strategies and key officers. The whole scenario drove me to seek a new combat procedure—psychological evaluation. I was lucky enough to find a counselor to help me get back on track, somewhat. She allowed me to voice my feelings; feelings of failure, despair anguish and a loss of desire to continue. For the first time in my life I had no desire to finish this battle.

The biopsy for cancer was in August of 2003—since I had prior cancer surgery and radiation I needed more testing for problems that could be looming. They were ordered and performed. I needed bone scans, chest and abdominal imaging to rule out any obstacles.

It was during a CT scan in October when the aneurysm was discovered. Surgery for the breast cancer was originally scheduled for 11/3/03 but was cancelled because of problems with the CT scan for the chest. I was admitted for the second surgery on 12/1/2003 and woke up to the doctor saying, "We couldn't perform surgery.

There was trouble inserting the tube down your throat". I was so sedated, but I cried out, "You're kidding?" Then I felt my chest and discovered both (well, 1 and a half) breasts intact. I fell asleep, when I awoke again, I asked what happened. "I thought I heard there was trouble with the tube insertion". Later

the doctor called and repeated there *was* trouble and they had to cancel surgery and use air bags to get me breathing again and resuscitated. The sedation took me again and I was unsure of what happened until I saw the doctor to reschedule surgery for December 30, after my throat and psyche had time to mend. I had to stay in ICU overnight for observation since I had been revived as to ensure all was ok with me and my throat.

I cannot comprehend the "tragedy and comedy" of the ordeals dealt me from these "terrorists within". First the wrong surgery in 1999 and the radiation ordeal. Now no surgery due to improper intubation and then still having to go through surgery the third time.

"Third times the charm", right??? Not in my case . . . after seeing the "job" the surgeons did, I felt like a freak—not because my breasts were gone, but because of the hideous surgery. To top off the disfigurement from surgery, I developed an infection (according to the doctors, it was again due to the radiation) on the left side. Well the infection was still there after 10 weeks. Then finally it seemed to be improving. I was beginning to really fear what was in store for me. I was doubting everything and everyone. My prayers were more like pleading.

I was very weak and fragile, but still had to the give the image of strength. My husband, children, mother, and sisters needed to know I'd be ok. If they only knew . . . I always considered myself strong—physically, mentally and spiritually. I felt as if my "army" had surrendered and left me as a captive. Left me to be mutilated and yet expected me to survive and come through as a "trooper".

I had the oncologist cancel twice: the 1st of March, now April 2. I am seething! I am so anxious, upset, confused, tired and lonely. Everyone thinks I am fine. "You look so good". "You sure bounced back quick." "I can't believe how well you've done!" Waiting to find out what, it any, treatment would be needed to demolish these terrorists was torture.

Those terrorists are bombing away at Camp Cerebral and Camp Heart. I am running out of ammunition. I try to fight but I think I'm losing. I can only fight so long alone. Everyone goes on their merry way (and it should be that way) . . . I should be ok now. I can drive, cook, do the laundry—I'm fine, everything is ok *in others eyes.*

Chemotherapy is still a major anxiety . . . along with this infection. The infection, I think, is just about licked, but I've never had anything hang on for

this duration, except hypertension. Twice a day to remove the bandage and see no, or very little, improvement is extremely hard.

Trying not to overdue as to not cause the lymphodema to worsen is another battle of those bogies.

I pray, if nothing else, that family, friends and inquirers get a true picture of what a cancer patient faces. The roller coaster is not exhilarating but taxing and exhaustive. The war drags on from each stage of treatment to the next.

Blessed are the patients that have friends or family that take the time to try to understand and are *really* concerned . . . not just, "how are you?" and then going on with trivial conversations, but really caring and try to help you cope. Maybe it's me, maybe I don't give anyone the chance. I'm so confused, so not wanting to be a bother, wearing the camouflage so they *can't* really see the war wounds, the depression, the shell shock. The song, **Someone to Watch Over Me,** is my theme song. How do I let go?? How do I confide?? I'm afraid spies will misconstrue my weakness for surrender . . . I'm not ready for that, but Lord, I can use a rest. A long peaceful sleep without any interruptions.

I understand I'm supposed to be at one of the nation's "best" hospitals. I truly realize all hospital staff is stretched and have heavy loads but, I feel, there is no excuse for my, or any other patient's, dignity being challenged. I've worked for 32 years in education which also is a service institution. I've been through the growth of the organization as the load kept increasing while the need grew but not the staff. I'm from the "old school" where you put the customer *first*. *Listen* to what they **say** they need and try to meet that need. If one is unable to meet that need, direct them to the correct department with an explanation (sometimes an escort).

It seems no one wants to *listen* . . . they have all the answers, put you through trial and error on a routine basis rather than *listen* to what you've been through. Too many problems go unsolved or medication is given for everything. Medication isn't always the answer—sometimes just reassurance or knowledge is needed to deal with a health issue. When medication or surgery **is** needed, **that** is when careful monitoring is needed by the physician or trained assistant. I've been given medication in doses way too high, it usually takes less to get me on the mend.

As I ramble on from one issue to another, the war continues. I am still waiting, after 3 months, to see the oncologist to establish the strategic maneuvers. Chemo seems to be the method of destruction. What degree? How long?? What

is the damaging outcome?? How long after treatment is expected recuperation time? Will there be complete recovery, or like radiation, will the residue last for years and cause further damage if other surgery is needed later?

Why do I have to do the research and think of all these questions? Why can't I just be called in and given all the info I need and be treated as a rational, thinking adult? Why must I keep track of every step along the way? Why do I have to fill out stupid questionnaires when no one reads them anyway? I can fill out a form, give it to the nurse, doctor or PA and I'll be darned if they don't ask me the very questions I just spent several minutes to answer—go figure.

There is just too much to comprehend, endure, and digest. I cannot, for the life of me, understand how we put our trust in these people who are "supposed" to be trained (especially) in the area of our need and still be so insensitive to what we are going through. Cancer has come a long way, thanks to technology and research. There is still so much unknown. So many differences in our fantastic human bodies. We all are treated as the same, when in fact, each person is different. At cancer support groups, it is so obvious. We go through the same process but come out different. Each person not only had a different physical makeup, but spiritual and mental as well. All of these, I found out, are most important in dealing with these issues as well as the fighting and healing.

Holy smoke—what else?? The latest is now a CT scan shows an aortic aneurysm that is enlarging . . . so guess what? I need an angiogram and possible surgery to repair it, *lucky me.*

The surgery for the kidney had to be postponed, due to the infection from the breast cancer, because both kidneys were needed to help with the infection. I had lymph nodes (20+) removed from each arm pit, so I needed the kidney to help fight. Chemo was ruled out because of the length of time elapsing because of problems. Radiation was ruled out because the first treatments in '99 left me so badly burned and infected.

My particular warzone keeps getting bombed. Bombshells and land mines all around: failed intubation attempts, infection, delays, aneurysms and angiograms. Walk carefully, follow orders, change strategies—report for inspections. Prepare for battle!!

So much to bear, still I can say—"I am Blessed". Everything is fixable. Thank God, I can have the angiogram if the aneurysm hasn't ruptured—still I am aghast, but ever so thankful.

The oncologist finally decides that due to the kidney issue, Femara, a cancer medication, would be started in lieu of chemotherapy. I will take this medication, probably, the rest of my life to help keep the cancer at bay.

I am at the point now that I just sit back and wonder. It is so unbelievable these "terrorists within". Well gear up—let's do this!! Better get a tank, these bumps in the road are too much for a regular vehicle. Orders are given even though they are sometimes hard to follow through. "Go to the lab with these papers." I get to the lab, "Go back to the doctor, we don't know what he wants." "We'll get the blood out of your hands", even though I was told no blood drawn or blood pressure readings from either arm—I don't know what to do. The less done to the arms will aid in preventing or lessening the chance of lymphodema.

The new *battle* is the renal aortic aneurysm. After two failed angiograms to insert a stint, I'm told I'll need a renal auto-transplant. This involves removing my left affected kidney, repairing the aneurysm and re-inserting my own repaired kidney in the pelvic area—AMAZING!

I get no guarantees: I could have a repaired kidney, one kidney working at less than present function, or no kidney. The other kidney on the right is operating at 1/3 capacity. The worse case scenario is the aneurysm could rupture before surgery and I could bleed to death.

OH, NO!! Those nasty terrorists! They have attacked my mother, how could they?? She does not deserve this—those "terrorists within" are cruel, heartless and insensitive. I just found out my mother has breast cancer and has to have surgery prior to my renal operation. I need a clone . . . another me so I can be there totally for my mom. How can I proceed, knowing my mom was at war, also. Too much to digest, I was so fragile (mentally) . . . my sister having her problems, now my mother and I with theses surgeries to gear up for. She was so brave and handled everything in her grand style.

*Prior to my "second" cancer surgery my youngest sister collapsed with diabetes—my first indication she had it. Picture this war zone: all the "normal" stresses of life: family, retirement, cancer for the second time, baby sister almost lost to diabetes, and now my mom diagnosed with breast cancer **plus** the renal surgery lingering in the background.*

Thank **GOD** for my husband, kids, grandkids, mother, sisters, brother and all my other family and friends. Thank God for the caring team of doctors I had and the counselor I had when I first found out I had cancer for the second time. So

many people to call on as needed. Despite all of the mishaps and postponements I was very pleased with 95% of my medical and psychological support.

I go in to the surgery pre-op session for preparation and instructions. The day of surgery I go to the hospital, the nurse comes in and asks for me. She then tells me surgery is cancelled because they just received two cadavers and *my surgeons* were needed for the patients anxiously awaiting organ transplants. I am numb, how many more of these ambushes can one endure, what next, why bother?? Please Lord, give me strength. Surgery was postponed for a week. AGONY.

My husband was so happy. He said he felt so good going home with me, *clueless.* He said he hated the other times he had to go home by himself and leave me in the hospital . . . he does not trust the hospital staff to do the right things. He has witnessed wrong medication being administered and other patients waiting for assistance when they need it. I understood how he felt, but I was dying on the inside. It is so hard to get yourself prepared for surgery, especially one so serious. I was so down, so deflated . . . not sure if I could gather the desire to prepare for this again. I know my strength was near its limit. My father was the one who would always instill the strength and the logical side to everything. He's no longer with us, what a void. Still I feel his being. It took everything and everyone I knew plus all my faith to help me through this . . . my army, my ammunition.

Finally, the renal auto transplant goes off without a hitch. The surgical team and recuperation team worked together and with me to assure me and give me instructions and physical therapy to get up and out. A week in the hospital and I get to go home. I am so relieved to get out of "fatigues" and into "civies" and back to "regular" life. Besides the usual pain and recuperation there seems to be no problems. My war has ended, except for the medication I need to take the rest of my life.

Once again, Life Is Good. I have no pending surgeries. I still cannot understand the workings of our marvelous bodies, but I truly appreciate them and the doctors and nurses that help with the mechanics and repairing of these exceptional machines.

—finis—

TIMELINE OF MEDICAL/ SURGICAL PROCEDURES

February 17, 1999   •   Cancer confirmed

February 25, 1999   •   Biopsy performed

March 16, 1999   •   Pre-Op

March 25-25, 1999   •   Left Breast Lumpectomy (Should have been left breast mastectomy)

December 1, 2003   •   Admitted for surgery, bilateral mastectomy (Sent home could not insert tube in throat)

December 30, 2003-
January 1, 2004   •   Bilateral mastectomy

January 3-4, 2004   •   Infection at surgical site presumed to be caused by radiation scars

*March 10, 2004   •   Baby sister collapses from sugar diabetes episode (first time finding out diagnosis)

March 30, 2004   •   Attempted immobilization of renal aneurysm (angiogram to insert stint)

April 12, 2004   •   2nd attempt (both attempts failed)

*April 22, 2004   •   Found out mother has cancer

*May 17-20, 2004   •   Mom admitted for right breast mastectomy

June 21, 2004   •   Pre-Op for left renal auto-transplant

June 23, 2004   •   Show up at hospital for scheduled surgery . . . sent home because two cadavers from an auto wreck came in and my doctors were needed for waiting organ transplant patients

June 29, 2004   •   Pre-op (2nd time)

June 30-July 7, 2004   •   Surgery for left renal auto-transplant (removal of left kidney from body, repair aneurysm re-insert kidney to pelvic area)

*   Family Medical Issues